UNDOLL

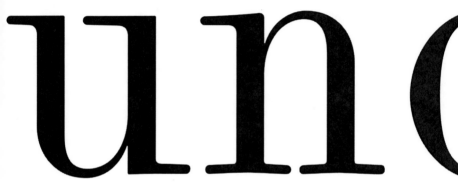

▶ YESYES BOOKS *Portland*

TANYA GRAE

UNDOLL © 2019 BY TANYA GRAE

FIRST EDITION

COVER PHOTO © INVISIBLESK / STOCK.ADOBE.COM

COVER & INTERIOR DESIGN: ALBAN FISCHER

ISBN 978-1-936919-53-6

PRINTED IN THE UNITED STATES OF AMERICA

LIBRARY OF CONGRESS CATALOGING-IN-PUBLICATION

DATA IS AVAILABLE UPON REQUEST.

PUBLISHED BY YESYES BOOKS

1614 NE ALBERTA ST

PORTLAND, OR 97211

YESYESBOOKS.COM

KMA SULLIVAN, PUBLISHER

STEVIE EDWARDS, SENIOR EDITOR, BOOK DEVELOPMENT

ALBAN FISCHER, GRAPHIC DESIGNER

DEVI GONZALES, MANAGING EDITOR

COLE HILDEBRAND, SENIOR EDITOR OF OPERATIONS

LUTHER HUGHES, ASSISTANT EDITOR & YYB TWITTER

AMBER RAMBHAROSE, EDITOR, ART LIFE & INSTAGRAM

CARLY SCHWEPPE, ASSISTANT EDITOR, *VINYL*

ALEXIS SMITHERS, ASSISTANT EDITOR, *VINYL* & YYB FACEBOOK

PHILLIP B. WILLIAMS, COEDITOR IN CHIEF, *VINYL*

AMIE ZIMMERMAN, EVENTS COORDINATOR

HARI ZIYAD, ASSISTANT EDITOR, *VINYL*

for my mother,
who taught me I could

Contents

THE INTENT TO BE LOST

Little Wekiva River

I want no evidence I am dirty.

All the fruit I picked, a dress full,
I let drop—
                    heavy shoes
on the heart pine floor.
Purpling under the skin, all
I thought I wanted:

the house with its backyard river,
swing set & sundial. Enough wild
bougainvillea sprang to be kept
overlooking the gate. Until now.
Sun leaving behind the live oak,
gnomon pointing—

me, stepping out of the dress.

The Last Bright Routes

Oblation

My gynecologist asks if others may watch.
I consent. Already numb, why not?
There should be an audience for this end.

An antiphon could be written in the hum
of machinery & whirr. My feet cold on metal
stirrups, my legs bent high in a squat,

I tune the sterile out. After today I won't
have a period, that punctuation I prayed for
at times will disappear. He tells me I will feel

some pressure, a little pinch, then dilate wide:
my cervix, my eyes. A laparoscopic camera
enters my universe, reveals on the monitor

a contrast to anatomy diagrams
of an inflamed red trumpet: a loft aglow—
carnations, white feathers, heaven

inside of me. The whole room presses
close to the screen. I turn my head away
as we tear the cradle down.

Matryoshka

One by one, they go
as I head to work & then the reverse. My mother made me
mise en abyme, standing between two mirrors.

I see ripples
in the pool, spilling out. Every choice goes on forever,
inscribing the vinyl record,

this galaxy carousel.
Sometimes I need to feel unique & responsible & alone.
In the car last week, my teenager said

it doesn't matter what I do—
she will be okay. *Déjà vu*. All the same words I told my mother
& my mother hers.

Like Fibonacci's parlor trick,
we rhyme ourselves, a strange loop of self-reference—
the vortex seen from above, a cut tree,

layers & layers of ringing.
My daughter wraps her arms around me & says good morning
before making her own eggs.

Proof enough
somewhere inside I am fetal (my mother
inside me & hers)

& the day goes on.

Mitochondrial Eve in Reverse

Everywhere holds a mirror.
Dimly, then face to face,
veins distill down, down
through the eye in the canopy.
There are plate glass panes
full of Indian blankets burning—
sudden meadows, clearings
to other doors & thresholds.
Full song, there are hinged doors
to rooms of passerines & rooms
of manufactured nests.
There is selection, the waiting,
& the house of the woods.
There is the house of my life.

Phalaenopsis

Unlike others, bright backyard trophies
that lean for a moment in the vase,

the orchid sits tall & lithe
waiting by the sink, dangle-legged

patience that outlasts perennials, a gift
shipped from an online hothouse

overnight. The known world is smaller—
diaspora turning, my dishpan fingers

search the gray, finding the last knife
from dinner. The art of an arrangement is

choosing wisely what thrives fasting, blossoms
without suburbia or baptism from the tap.

Wean, though the plastic tag advises submersion,
so the bloom will last.

Ripe

1

The last pomegranate, a fat fist
comb with bloody honey

sits ovarian on the countertop—
a pregnant pause of the paring knife

on the edge of the breadboard
by the Pyrex bowl & spoon.

Amy shrugs from the stereo:
You know that I'm no good.

And my children mill in & out
of the kitchen, peckish.

2

I learned to bury my mouth
throat-deep & pulse-suck
every aril free, sleeve-wiping
juice from my skin, savage
& sticky, how desire ends.

3

Release, the de-seeding trick:
I score the skin's circumference
& work my fingertips in, gently
pulling hemispheres apart

& then hold each half face-down
& with a wood spoon, whack
the backside until red-purple
arils ring the bowl like hail.

4

On the news tonight at eleven:
The fall's dominion over the world
& the regalia orb of the apple—

how one bite, in hindsight, brings
a punishment for knowing. Watch
fresh-out-of-the-garden Eve

turn ready to kick Adam's ass:
An extended hand is not a gun.
No one made you eat.

5

I fall asleep on the couch
& dream Morpheus drops in
offering a choice of cosmotinis:

Apple to go out, pomegranate
deeper in. Either way, girl—
it's your sin.

6

Some seasons arrive late
like epiphany, regret. Yes,

Persephone with those seven seeds,
screaming *Mother—*

hair half-ripped out, narcissus
still tight in hand—*why?*

& I can't get my damn self
out of bed?

7

One eye open, one eye closed
          looking at the clock. *Mom!*
Something misplaced. The morning
          shuffle/scuttle/race/pace
                    to get out the door, a blink
          of calm & cue the tenor—*Damn it!*
Someone moved my keys! Retrace
          your steps to what you lost.
          Visualize when you held it last.
                    Walk back far enough & you'll find it
unless it's gone.

Waiting

Just as I heard his truck on the driveway,
the glass slipped from my hand, vertigo

like I've never had it. Knowing how
the night will go: his three-minute hate

disguised as hello, no kiss & two beers.
He'll sit in that chair & rail the evening news

when the war is already here.

Stupefied

words leave no bruise   I connect the zings

watching twenty-dollar shampoo   drain

     overhead   a pop-up balloon   floats

     cursor blinking   waiting for the edit

     a subroutine runs   & searches the mess

dumping random drawers   in a mad rummage

finding the remote   the prodigal sock

     choice retorts   of hours ago

     take Faulkner & his darlings   *shring*

     how to reconstitute   a scrambled egg

     collect the power berries   pink blue red

& medicate like Pac-Man   *nom nom*   yes

here in the shower   numb in the flow   of white noise

     my filaments tangled   a rat-combed wild

     gaskets could blow   a shock   wave   out

     the crown intestine unwound   in one cleanse

     erasing marginalia   of wrongs   guilt

fattening food   for the last goat   penned

     standing fast   in this rain   holding

     just cause   a thing is said

     doesn't make it so

To Come Undone

My mother used to say lipstick was best
        manners, praised the importance of putting on
a good face. Add to the list: the padded bra,
        slip & girdle clothes-pinned to the line.
How the nakedness of women without makeup
        used to shock me, their blemishes & pores.

Be a lady everywhere except the bedroom.

But that braless summer my aunt didn't
        shave armpits, legs, anything, too much skunk
running wild in her appearance, we sang
        "American Girl" before she met the Wolfman
who hid her behind dark glasses. Face dolled up
        like *Redbook*, how she bent herself in his moods.

Beauty is skin deep, but ugly is to the bone.

My father used to call my mother's name
        & she'd drop everything & go. It startled me
the urgency of something wrong, misplaced—
        his keys, a shoe. But those affairs he had
for years, after she gave up college to marry,
        fueled three degrees at choke-down speed.

Make sure you can take care of yourself.

I learned to say no & outlast the silence,
        tired of hours, contortions to please.
I cut my own hair & let myself go.
        Those bare-faced women I used to study,
whose eyes scolded mine, knew one day
        I'd shrug at the mirror & say, *So?*

Facebook Sonnet

Someone thinks I'm beautiful again
            & likes posts of my day, comments.

I stifle smiles & feel uncontainable—
            bungeed off ether & the interplay.

Punch drunk in this blue-sky space
            a rush of the past, the in-between,

whole chapters, I open annuals
            & albums from storage. His change

in status: single. Papers in hand
            this backlit man heaves toward

the kite's trailing end: *What if?*
            That butterfly. My youngest lights

onto my lap, *Who's that?*
            A key turns the lock. I log off.

What's Bottled Breaks

                    Not at first,
like the letter that doesn't come, but the one that does
& makes no sound as it holds the room.
                             This morning, rain
taps on the sill & words rise to mind & fall like swells
on the piano & never cease to surprise, at least in Florida
with its riptides & surrender. *Sunshine State.*
                             Between beaches,
just two days ago, I considered the world mapped. Today
the roads are rearranged & the cities mislabeled.
Maybe the state is broken, or my own is
                     or yours—
people losing direction & sense, unbecoming themselves
in pulled feathers & song. Even the resident mockingbird
cleans her wings, shrugs.
                     What magnetism drives this?
Maybe the new moon stirs the sun & we'll have hurricanes
in winter. What sound would that make?
                      A whisper in your ear
bring a rise? I've imagined falling in love again,
something I no longer thought possible, but
in this crescendo unresolved, you—
                  again & again.
What are the odds? I read a story yesterday of a boy
who found a message in a bottle
                decades at sea.

The Unfaithful Housewife

after Federico García Lorca, translated by Conor O'Callaghan

no one led me to the river
         & I was not a virgin
     because I had a husband & you
those long July weekends
         in Mobile you asked me to stay
     the street lights weren't on yet

as I parked at the restaurant
         areolas electric body
     heat diffusing perfume
& the cotton of my jeans
         you in your fine linen suit
     table votive with its aureole

of gold the haze your eyes
         I forgot my life so fast
     eight hours from the river
past the longleaf pines
         scrub palms & billboards
     after two glasses of pinot

I let down my hair
         you took off your tie
     & reached for my hand

my need to kiss you
                your cocksure play
            no coffee no dessert

nothing in all of Florida
                has half the sweetness
            that night you might
have harnessed the winds
                off the Gulf of Mexico
            winged unbridled mind

I play back the murmurs
                my body still bitten you
            pulled me from the river
& tangled bougainvillea
                married yes but
            fallen & already yours

Duchess

a found poem

If you would just be a better wife.
                    a better mother.
                    like my mother.
                get off the computer.
                    off the phone.
                have dinner ready when I get home.
If you would just stop spending money.
            just wash my clothes.
                clean the _____.
                pay attention to the kids.
                stop spoiling the kids.
                    taking their side over mine.
If you would just rub my hair.
                stop playing with the dog.
                rub my back.
        would just put the book down.
                touch my _____.
            just blow me, then go to sleep.
If you would just help me with the business.
                stop acting like my boss.
        would just leave the business alone.
                get a job.
    you   make it all about your job.

realize your check doesn't pay the bills.
If you would just see I'm not one of your students.
see you're just like your mother.

you   make it all about you.

so depressed.

such a nutbag.
If you would just talk about it.

spend time with me.

stop talking; I'm trying to watch TV.

just try harder.

be content.

just change, problem solved.
If you would just act like you give a damn.

care more about what I think than _____.

stop pissing me off.

saying FUCK all the time.

just fuck me.

initiate.
If you would just not bait me & make me yell.

stop yelling, then I wouldn't yell.

just pay attention to what I'm saying.

not be such a bitch.

just let it go.

grow up.
If you would just—never mind; it's like talking to a fucking wall.

just die.

stay.

The Google Earth Effect

Visible from space, my house
sits on a little river, or at least
from satellite view where I see
the vertebraed arrangement
of lots & streets. A red-hot
balloon pinpoints the spot
I've been lost all these years.
Call it *Still Life with Joystick.*
In this virtual diorama, I fly low
where nothing moves, no cars,
no cats, no one watering a lawn
& shrink back to play home.
If I were a stranger, I might
picture the people inside
but the door is closed & blinds
drawn & there's no hint at all
of yelling. Who understands
unless they're in it? I find myself
rotating the view straight above
to look for the all-seeing eye
or at least the sky on that day
& pan up & out & over & away.

Patience as a Force

               Tie a knot & hold on—
pretend minutes are mile markers on the road.

Drive home from work as heat rises from the asphalt,
cars, two lanes of traffic you absently cut off.

    Virtue: doubt: a ring of fire, sound the alarm.
    How long before this pariah triggers the pyre,
    the whole system swarming out, piling its logs
    & kindling, quick to light? One Mississippi.
    Two Mississippi. Three Miss[a]—

Pick up the kids & listen as they replay their day.
When they bicker over the radio, tune out, away.

    Plausible deniability:
    no need to mention the subject.
    As anonymous is to name
    infinitive is to action.

    To stay: MAN-Ē-RE
    To flee: FUG-Ā-RE
    To feel: SENT-Ī-RE

SENTI, SENTIAM—

Home around the corner,
first you look for his truck.

Mad lib:
"The problem with you is _____.
You should _____. If you would
just _____, then everything would be better.
We're never going to be okay
until you _____."

See the half-moon wane above the door. Inhale & enter.
Let the dogs out, make dinner.

see the girl make a calendar   of graph paper
            her scrolled wings   to eighteen press against

the window watch her   Scotch tape months
            to years a rosary   of counting days

does all prayer have   an end in mind
            navigate   with scissors shear

latitude &   longitude the promise of
            land   the crow flies time introvert

Check homework for the youngest, who has yet to ask why
the couch is Dad's bed. Move small, move slow.

under pressure constantly moving   mountains calve into the sea
under its own weight a glacier forms   of friction of crack & crevasse
where snow outlives the melt   the weight of water the speed
the slow deform & flow of stress   the slow deform & flow of stress
the weight of water the speed   where snow outlives the melt
of friction of crack & crevasse   under its own weight a glacier forms
mountains calve into the sea   under pressure of constantly moving

Like counting knots on a rope & holding—

Oblivion is the place time forgets. Suburbia, Hell. Even Odysseus took a number in purgatory. Hope is another name. Solitary confines the condemned beyond wait. Mind in a house, words in static, were they said? Who listens these days? Ninety-nine, ninety-nine bystanders against the wall. Downtown on Church Street, a sun-leathered woman moves her cart past locals, past tourists, a live erasure in a grimy Magic t-shirt, she hums: YOU DON'T SEE ME—

wait & *count* & *breathe.*

There are Days

He doesn't care
what his words hit inside.
I hear my grandmother's
memory exhale *girl*—

her long, throaty curve
clatters the windowpane,
makes my eye twitch.
Mister, you have no idea

the patience I house
drips my walls, ambers
like Smyrna bees
filling a comb—

that furtive knit against
what bruises fruit & space.
Thou shalt not murder
but a hard ball cracks

where no one sees.
There's no count,
days when there are
just too many.

Lethe

For all the fish, the little blessings that I missed,
maybe I should just thank you. We can leave
the dress behind that didn't fit or fly to a new city
& wear the metropolis as our skin. Things happen,
how one love becomes another. In seasons, maybe
it's okay to remember how I lived multitudes of lives.
Where does oblivion begin? Years I tried to forget?
And be reborn? Not as a naiad. No. I want feathers
& dark. Let me be the hunter. According to Virgil,
I'm almost ready. But if long to stay, I should know
how I got here. How I—Have I been drinking
your water so long I've erased whole passages?
Maybe I'll forget. I forget everything these days.

Rewind

I look for what keeps me here,
that first love & breathlessness
my therapist compares to crack—

that high when I don't give a fuck,
when I feel like I've won, when I am
solid & safe & lightness, that *yes*.

To stay here is Hollywood & celluloid
reel, flammable, wound so tight
a fingernail can't wedge between

then & now, a spool of mind
I replay when nothing catches,
when my prayer beads move

under thumb faster & faster, when
the bike pedals outpace the chain,
when all the plates I'm spinning drop

& ring the house to silence—
that flood of light
when the movie burns.

A Dark Red Season

Loaded Noir

In the final climax of the marriage,
Joyce points the .38

at Maurice, the sour mash belligerent,
cigarette smoke face

leaning in yellow porch light,
his body shimming the screen door,

his forehead pressing against the jamb.
He eyeballs the scene through the slant:

his woman backlit, holding ground
beside the last suitcase & my mother,

at nine years old. He soaks it all in
& wrings out a dry smile, croons:

Baby, you ain't gonna use it.
Why you gotta be so mean—

I imagine their panic, the crawl
space of the living room air.

My mother says it was spirit sense:
when he walked back to his car,

she jumped & locked the bolt
& saw him get his shotgun

before they ran out the back,
Joyce's Bel Air out of view,

already packed, Maurice's voice
rising over Curtis Street:

Baby, I don't wanna use it.
Why you gotta make me so mean?

The Line of a Girl

1

At sunrise, our caryatid
stands at the kitchen window
& white embroidered curtains
diffuse daylight into her glow.

I study her silhouette:
the load-bearer, the muse,
my grandmother as Atlas, yet
Smyrna moves outside this

woman—within her history
another South, different endings
my child mind can't perceive.
She is a belle smoldering

with cigarette. Her drawn lines
surrendered, illuminate
& sear. Scythe. Burning. Joyce,
the lighthouse of hours, the late.

2

In the afternoons, I draw close
& practice reading books aloud.
She listens for a lilt, even in prose,
signifying import with her brow,

generations of correction
so I will speak well, genteel,
the diction of illusion.
My savored prize, her smile,

exhales the gray as she grinds
a filter into her wedding silver
ashtray; white flags on gristled
embers bear her wreck, red stain.

3

She fills her glass & it empties
& again. Days I watch until
my mouth is dry. I am off to play;
she is lost in sight, the undertow

of entertaining oneself when lonely
& not alone—all the comfort is outside.
I spend hours underneath the mimosa,
the fern lace light of its shade, jazz-

handed pink in constellation.
From wherever, I am her Black-eyed
Susan here. Wide acres over it all, free.
A girl running. *Jesus, can you see me?*

I feel so small—not as little
as a thrush or the ruby-throats
tongue-deep in the honeysuckle
with furious wings, not easy to be.

But she was that sudden goddess
amid small-town bourgeoisie,
out of air. An invisible net—
is it so intangible, the life

versus living? This, her way out:
arranged, comfortable years
with a gentle man, without want.
What of a settled home, why fear?

4

Dear heart—the same words
of my mother, the appearance
of elevation, the right tone,
the pleasing smile. Beauty cries

over a bitten lip, nails dug deep
into a fisted palm. Years later, this
same bed I've made, this lie I keep,
summons her presence, uncalm.

Does my tremor wrench the line—
that silver cord, that river
of provenance between us?
I feel her in the curtain weight,

the sail, the ballast. My house reels
adrift as the floors settle & moan,
the walls, my head spinning. *Jesus—
do you feel it too?*

Portrait of a Clarion

the night   before Joyce died   I dreamed she passed
over my bedroom   hours south   of her own bed
nimbus flying   with orchestral arms   & prone
the coal-tressed starling   of her twenties   a sylph
vocalizing   a hurricane squall   throwing doors wide
she was no longer   my grandmother   in a housecoat
wrestling sleep   grinding her teeth   down to buds
metastasis   mocking her marrow   she was
a terrible sight   one breasted   & winged
a seraph in victory   the dirge   the descent
in the phonograph   of my ear   Billie Holiday
singing: *angels*   *have no thought*   *of ever*
returning you   she willed   to hear
I wasn't waking   but somehow   in fugue
watching her   watch me   I woke falling
the wrenching jolt   the flutter of her   no longer
there   wrinkled   under the wake
& stranglehold   of that   twenty-third May
when   the call came   no answer just

Magnolia

Who can summon back the running water
when Joyce cradled the weight of my head

in her hand? Playing beauty parlor in her kitchen,
our summer ritual, with my body outstretched

across the countertop, my legs bent to avoid the stove.
I hated when she would scrub too hard

working through my tangles & felt I'd outgrown
her grand mothering. The flared sun I resisted:

her irises, hazel green in morning light, the slant
arch of her brow. Even now when I bend backward

in the shower, closing my eyes to avoid the sting
of lather & fury, my fingers work through strands

that will never feel quite as clean.

Letter to My Embryo, Evolving

You could be anybody, kind & brilliant,
sitting next to me on a plane, headphones on,

dreaming about Thanksgiving. Your unwritten
face wears the smile of old masters; inside,

you're the sketchbook's turned page. But
sometimes I panic & want to wake you

to turn back & conscientiously object—
as if you enlisted at some karmic weigh station,

given the hard sell: *Just think of the enlightenment!*
It's almost 4 AM & your future glares at me

in a wild, half-woken way. The dog is snoring
& you are kicking softly, but mostly the world is

quiet. Soon I will fall back to sleep & let hours keep
these concerns. Forgive this burden

& wrench this life
for its surprising specks of joy.

Sunday School

our preschool teacher leads *this little light of mine*
        & what can wash away my sins & asks me to recite
    the memory verse as she leans her ear I whisper
        be kind to one another & claim a star I want to be
so good even better never the one put in the corner
        for being sassy we learn God in His glory made a garden
    then Adam then Eve & told them not to eat the fruit
        from that tree & how the snake said eat anyway
because what good is not knowing I'd eat that apple too
        it's so hard to be good our teacher prays the offering
    Amen & hands a daisy beach pail to the cow-licked boy
        & sends him around to collect our quarters & dimes
& invites us forward to accept salvation & smiles
        when I raise my hand *who made God* her face stones
    her *pardon me* so shrill my eyes cut to the window & bright
        tissue square collage a breeze across the pines
the water tower stands as we sing *praise God from whom*
        all blessings flow then tidy & say goodbye the church
    bus delivers me home I swing open the screen door
        peel down to my slip & bare feet & run outside to lie
heathen on the grass under the Mississippi Flyway my arms wide
        miles high a gospel of blackbirds ministers away

South Charlene

Those months I stayed out till dark,
boys on my street plucked wings
off damselflies, primary & metallic
like matchbox cars & pocket heroes.
Bees melted in their mason jar chemistry
& ants magnified into wisps of smoke.
Little cruelties, that carnage, torsos
writhing on sidewalks—their attention
turned & sent my girl legs running.
Idiots, the lot, but gods of summer
& our block, the boundary so small.

Why Not Minot

The welcome arch read *Only the Best Come North* & my parents laughed
tongue-in-cheek at another cross-country Air Force move. In fifth grade,
I learned about America & the Dakotas & the Cold War & elections as
Reagan won office. My teacher called him *a warmonger* & at dinner my
mother said, *Don't worry,* as my father's face hardened. He said, *We keep
the world safe.* But that winter a whiteout hit & erased all but the edges of
duplexes & Dundee Drive, like a snow globe shaken, a diorama in which
mastodons would have lived: glaciated Northern plains, a drifting surface
wind, green borealis ghosting the stars. And just before dark I took a walk
further than allowed & tromped a snowdrift over the high fence separating
the base from miles of wheat fields in every way until horizon was a blur.
My breath suspended in whorls, in sound. A half-mile out alone, I looked
back—at lights turning on one by one, at my steps, where they ended—
unaware of long-range missiles & fatigued men deep beneath my feet
working twenty-four-hour shifts holding an imaginary line.

Here is Somewhere

just as late sun bends the edge
of Arizona   west light climbs through the window
    &warms my face   running in Tennessee   wild
    blackberry fields   grass brushing my thighs
    shirt full of summer   blossom honey
    another house spinning   in mid air
    seven homes   in thirteen years
    repacking   unpacking   myself
    books   posters   pinned maps
    a dresser mirror   flowering over questions
    my *looks white but*   not Cherokee
    my father's face   passing   erased
    my mother's Irish skin   who exactly is what
    the doubt   against the push
    to fit   not looking
    beneath my feet
    an exponential line
    of ancestral mothers
    holding ground
    Here I am
    wherever here is
    anyway

Post-Hellenic

Hair spills over my face as he glides
                my cutoffs to my thighs, all Coppertone
        & cream. Straight from mythology, he is
                one of the junior gods, where I'm an extra

in the scene. He crosses the caution, hand
                glossing lips, tongue & ticklish, my hips
        confessing fireworks all at once—
                the fourth of July. Early independence,

this taste. *More*—wings, electric, titillation
                of what a girl can do, how to turn it,
        serve it—to a boy in an Eagles jersey
                & button-flys. He finger-combs his look

& leans back against the bleachers. Beautiful
                boys without brains are disappointment,
        the *whoa*—to fasten my shorts & float
                feather-light, that subtle tallness

that comes on & lingers against the glow,
                the half-grin, the horizon. Here he ends,
        but there are highways, towns,
                other names I'll forget.

Third Wave

When my mother sat at our table
for late hours of statistics homework,

biting the corners of her lips,
I felt prophecy swell without translation.

I studied, taking comfort in the closest
I could get: my mother brawling—

head down, grinding each equation,
my whole life set in her jaw.

Gaslight

At the late-night pool party, someone flips a switch.
~~I am~~ the stumbling girl in the hot pink beach towel
~~who passes out~~ falls asleep in a bedroom
while trying to recover & wakes screaming

& you *shhhhhh*—
to calm her down, fumbling

for light & then leave her to ~~fall apart~~
piece ~~herself~~ the night together, until

you reappear with reinforcements, two

older girls who know you ~~I thought I did~~
assume this is ~~rape~~ her first time & ~~I'm~~ she's just scared.
Standing at the door, you look so ~~innocent~~ damned.

~~Maybe it's because my dad is a Chief Master Sergeant~~
~~& you're an airman & an adult & I am sixteen.~~
You've been such a good friend.

~~Shelia & Kathy left me because you offered to drive~~
~~me home. I trusted you & drank that line of shooters:~~
~~lick the hand, pour the salt, lick, drink, suck, slam.~~
She must have looked like she wanted it

~~bent over & throwing up. Why else would you~~
~~call my boyfriend back in town & tell him I fucked you?~~
~~I'll never get over it. You said he wasn't good for me~~
& you did her a favor.

~~Maybe I did you one by hating myself~~
~~for years, not realizing you might have gone to jail.~~
~~Look at the ways I punished myself.~~
How did she look

listening to you all—before she left
torn in that part that said ~~die~~ goodbye, thanks

for having her & for the ride.

Rizzo's Song

I sang full voice in my girl pink room,
  driving my mother crazy. I wore out
    the vinyl, the irony, the foreshadow
of my teenage role, a mezzo like Stockard Channing
    playing low, *There are worse things I could do*—
  How I hated you at first, until I didn't,

our high school operetta no different—
    reading *Romeo* & *Juliet* & watching Zeffirelli,
  me sneaking out my window to catch midnight
movies at AMC & *Rocky Horror* in the Grove,
    the era of John Hughes & us skipping school
  at Crandon & coming home tan & catching hell

& fire & holding hands at Dadeland & Bayside
    & The Falls & hallways & all the notes & cards
  & bears & you teaching me how to drive stick
in your dad's old Karmann Ghia & kissing slow
    & playing games & the way you cried laughing
  at something I'd say & the sex at Alice Wainwright,

even Vizcaya & our Renaissance. The splendor—
    no one else understood our moon phases & tides
  like pregnant & then not & the hospital & my parents

& your parents & you at boot camp & long-distance
              engaged & that pool party & the rape of that call
       & breaking up & other boys & me being so aloof

& never getting back to that place when we could
              just lie together spooned in your room. Why
       could I never say the truth? That half bottle
of Percocet & wine coolers to fly my Malibu
              upside down through a tomato field. *I can feel*
       & I can cry. A fact I bet you never knew—

that first kiss at Ocean Reef on your birthday,
              or sitting in chemistry, thinking I didn't see you
       in the bleachers while I cheered or in a crowd
or that first time underneath the water tower,
              the dew already rising, the dog star on the hem
       of night's skirt pulled down for morning.

As Faithful as His Options

We are expected to be pretty and well-dressed until we drop.
—Edith Wharton, *The House of Mirth*

Imagine a circle jerk of cigared & brandied men
      who lament the collar is slipping—*a screw, a cog*
in the great machine—There are no jokes.
      If literature has taught me anything, it's that

people evolve but repeat their mistakes.
      Who calibrates virtue? In the wake of Sim's candor,
Lily Bart haunts me: the undertaste of feminine
      commodity, the lever edge of laude to laudanum.

Half the trouble in life is caused by pretending
      there isn't any. Take an object: Question its beauty—
in form, in line, in color. Does it bring you joy?
      A trail in the dust reminds *once she's talked about*

she's done for; & the more she explains the worse it looks,
      how furniture is rearranged, how chairs are
pulled out or taken away. *There's no turning back*—
      Would another look as fine in the same position?

Perhaps the seat as better empty as warm?

    Remember the punchline: *your old self rejects you*
& *shuts you out*—Lawrence is too late: Lily's hand still,
    the empty bottle sideways by the nightstand—

the air sick-sweet of her waiting, that violent
    rise in the bile of my throat.

The Intent to Be Lost

Newlywed

Marc Chagall, *La Promenade*, 1918. Oil on canvas.

Open her hidden hand.
On the hillside above Vitebsk,
above the blanket set with wine,
that is, by design, a world set apart,
her eyes fold his best clothes aside.
Her violet dress lighter from his touch,
she looks back at his wide-happy smile.
Before the quilted landscape, their hands
hold to wrists like doves as the wind lifts,
wind that pulls as a muse: *More time, more—*
against the rumpled down of clouds: *Let go—*
Her eyes beg for gravity, her skin with his, her body
upon the grass. In midair, she turns, a volta
against the birdless sky. Marc stands outside
this vignette with Bella, his ecstasy intact,
his bird in hand & blurs the air to heighten
the fore through a waltz of refraction.
The unhappy town steps back quietly
& happiness is the day, is the theme,
as if given dominion, reign. His
outstretched hand paints her
forever from flying away.

Black Iris Sonnet

Knees worn green, hands clayed
with sand & muck, I wear my life
pursuit, no less a bruise. Why persist
in bed making, in sweat & stain
for idylls in spring? What emerges
from such ambition? My palm cradles
each seed to soil, each amphibious
heart, the primordial hope held
in a three-chambered pod to throb
& suckle & thrust. The organic engine
muscles Demeter's alchemy
under bedsheets of myth & pang,
a knuckled promise held tight.
There is no vanity in birth.

Wuthering

I am another man's wife—
a fact that eats me
in small bites, zoned out
as the microwave seconds
count down. I think of him
when my husband feels
the need, wrecks me
where I've tucked myself
in [a contortionist's feat]
to stare at the assault—
how a lie devours daylight
& years. How long past no
does the hole implode?

Tomb of the Wrestlers

Rene Magritte, *The Tomb of the Wrestlers*, 1960. Oil on canvas.

When I stand undressed in front of you,
you unshame me in that space,
the home you are, every room full
with Magritte's rose. What is mirage?
How minds entwine & race
through walls like the warp of stars—
volume with no end, no containment—
hothouse in the abstract, inside
one florescing leap for the edge, alive.

In Elixir

In the bottom of a mason jar, anyone,

                mermaid or sailor,

can get snared in the ether with feathers, ice
& the silver line of hooks.

             How a lure intoxicates

under its dopey moon. I forget discretion, to shelter my thoughts
with a smile. Transparent creatures of the ocean

                      wear no expression

in their lulling way. If we pretend they're benign & don't sting,
they don't dissolve

          the fullness of Pandora's *pithos*

mid-throat to say what we want isn't what is, but if it was
we'd be immortal.

         Shine can blind a person

in one drink & sink the dark right into their deep.
How our passions maroon us.

             The slow wake

to curse thirst. An hourglass of sugar turns to salt—
a mouthful of pinion, rudder, course.

                  We enter naked

& take on form. There are no wings while we walk—
folded, dormant, beating

          disguised in our pulse.

Waterline

A body is sixty percent
ocean & the rest sediment.

A ship at sea bears load to
the plimsoll, its safe burden.

If a limescale fresco remains
to mark history, the flood's rise

& fall, without me jumping in
to live it again, the scene

where I don't wear a diving bell,
where I free-dive grasping

one breath—
there's no line for that,

only the primal sense
of treading water in bed.

Cage Sonnet

the road offers right or left   & miles either way
what if I go there   here   or turn toward more
each step a hello   & goodbye   or to stay
nerve song   of my feet   the tenor
hymns of want   making do   of someday
& into night   places too vast   to ignore
the weight of low   on eggshells   the fog of gray
the world beats   different   outside this door
I can't abide the house   anymore   to please
little choices are made   windows open & shut
some rooms I brighten   & some I just survive
places   years   stagnate   with a quiet ease
while the best groove   can turn suddenly   to rut
walk out   & run full run   an arson of why

After Fifteen Years

Before a bad storm
Florida sky is an overripe mango.

I smell ions & night jasmine.

He plays "Hard Habit to Break"
on his way home from work &

I toss his birthday cake in the river.

The Last Silueta

*I have been carrying out a dialogue between the landscape
and the female body (based on my own silhouette).*
—Ana Mendieta

another morning fight
out of nowhere
another migraine
zigzagging the edge
of my eyes I close
the door to dress
catch hold of myself
       in the window
diaphanous & twin
dimensioned a nude
transposed with oak
melding navel & clit
viburnum & blue-red
bougainvillea spilling
the sill
       a *silueta* Ana
I've been praying
not to wake now you
angel in my mind's eye
with arms raised above
the city in the same

       painting light
before neighbors report
the yelling your insides
gnawing out the dream
       were you facing
when the sky reversed
thirty-four floors form
attenuating gravity grasp
your
       cadmium red
that little voice
that said
he would never

Mall at Millennia

track lights flare in the reflection
of a store window in the middle
of a sprawling mall in the City
Beautiful the atrium the trine a
teddy beside a push-up beside a
corset under angels' downed wings
in the hermetic display of perfume
of violin of velvet of want of what
grinds a body in gravity that simply
is even with stage & contour & pin
& tuck the glint without glitter
in the vaulted air absorbing its
clientele in each erased face in
the curvature of a fiberglass mold
in neophytes shaped of opinions
in packaging in parts in desire to
appeal in the eyes milling past
the food court & kiosks holding
themselves together in the selfie
uncertain in the pout in the
reflections cast in silver sand in
their shift of perception in my shift
store light glares

Closing Stepford

A small disclaimer: METAMORPHOSIS CAN BE IRONIC. Just initial here: _____. Great! Today's the first day of your best wife, best life! Let's go through your options:

Her hair, no longer stringy, will be fistfuls of silk. Brown? Are you sure? Okay, more mink than mom. You checked breasts as a concern—not to worry. How about an upgrade? Feel free to double E, tip-tilted

toward the sun. Tan legs, smooth feet, toes polished candy bright. She's always set to go. Forget shrill, forget no & wait 'til I show you volume control—the mute! Her mouth won't spew anything

from its sweet supple bow. When you speak, her eyes follow then avert. This isn't a spell—this is science! We can't wait for evolution, right? A good wife lives to please. No worries of grad school or menses or militancy.

Her mood default is doe. Or, if you prefer: perky, sultry, awe. That's not all—her friends are programmed the same. No sisterhood revolution. And the remote—it's universal! When you focus on her eyes, you

never have to doubt. She's not faking it for you.

If Barbie had a Brain

No, I mean if Barbie could talk,
she would tell you she's starved

for more than an eyeful's attention,
ass clenched tight, kind of holding.

Asphyxiated from sucking in, waiting
to stop the tiptoe, she objects

to being posed, back aching, ending
horizontal & naked, because

her clothes are too much of a hassle—
your illusion undressed. She knows

about the curb, where your things tend
to end & wants you to know

doll patience is painted.

Anatomically Correct

To God: How does anything change?

To myself: Write your way out.

I draw a line down the body   through the life.
I weigh consequences   & chart the house filled
with children   grafted debt & belongings.
Conjoined   how does one divide? These nights
are ripe with croaking   & drawn blinds rest
their case against noise   how memory blurs
our present   how we grapple how we're stuck.
I've inked this scalpel.   Complex run amok.
Yes, your Madonna-whore   healer excavator mind
set with an ax   & too many words to steady a pen.
Watch my chest.   I'll close my eyes & cut.

Lot's Wife Leaves Suburbia

si vis pacem, para bellum—
If you want peace, prepare for war.

Today I slammed the door so hard
the house fell behind me.

If any ring remains, of rubble
& consequence, my salt heart

agape, an *oh* to construct
the shape of the whole just before—

This was my war:
I did not shrink to fit

remarks landing around me,
in me, fire almost out

when fury came, the seam rip
of thunder, a rush of mothers

howled through my mouth
burst wide. The mothy swarm

blackened the room
hurling tables, smashing plates,

launching the oven & washer
through the window—

The wife life I lived laid waste
& the shock of it rang.

The door was the end as in the day
of Lot & the host & hail fire,

except I refused to look back
& kept walking.

Not the Myth

The Path of Non-Attachment

I was born in a cross-fire hurricane.
—The Rolling Stones

At 4:54 AM
Andrew totaled my car, leveled the house

& destroyed nearly every piece of furniture.
The day before, I could see the spiral coming

on the news. Everyone said ride it out. Batten down.
Buy water & canned food, but the shelves were bare.

I bought wine & crackers & black cherry seltzer.
I glazed, predictions tightening, my head swimming

room to room. I didn't tape or board the windows
or light Lucky Maria candles. I couldn't think to pray.

I packed my mother's Amelia Earhart suitcase
with photos & journals I couldn't replace

& left Homestead, unclear what must be kept
or let go, the way we marry & give ourselves away.

If only each disaster announced itself, a siren
warning of the storm we won't survive. Whose life

can be replaced like new? More to have, to hold
but years? I stumble on the surest things I know.

And standing at an airport carousel
in another city, I watch an unclaimed bag

pass again that someone somewhere
feels better lost than found.

A Sting Hovers in My Window

Unmoved by my presence, the wasp
works one end of her nest to the other.

The lintel's shade elides the screen
between our dwellings as the cross breeze

carries the bark of squirrels, annoyed
by this blur of proximity. Somehow

right here, I realize the singularity of living—
the Little Wekiva flows behind this house

into a greater river, an exhale set free.
The whole world simmers low & for change,

how orchids rehearse inside their bulbs
& this mother keeps building, unalarmed

by late season warmth
with no hope for spring.

Doll, House

There is a home where I shrink inside
to fit every room. More out of body

than furniture, but I have been that too,
posable in the kitchen & bath,

tub filled to the brim, shower falling.
Remember? I have been the carpet

& Queen Anne chair, coffee table set
for you, dresser, with belts & ties.

Trope the bed, to rule with no rules, king
spread pulled wide. What is a realm

with windows painted shut, sun slanted
& the view, a daydream? I never knew

I had a smallest self & wasn't looking
when I forgot I was alive.

Mirror, Mirror

Men will crack your glaze
even if you leave them before morning.
   —Brenda Shaughnessy, "Postfeminism"

I don't wear my mother's body, but there's no use
sneaking around the house, this gingerbread
pre-fab, forest-scented with vanilla snow. Punch

drunk on fairy tales. Non-ascetic. I've been
two kinds of romantic: hungry poet emoting
in a pack, youth-high on asterisk endorphins. Both

strung out, marauding baskets & snacks, preying
on predators that never see it coming, quick ravels
of spindle-wit lingerie & perfume in verse. I go on

being voracious. Hand-fed fantasia, baby doll &
vermouth. Yes, there are two kinds of people: virgins
& wolves. Apple wide for poison or the truth. Ah

the bitch of one bite, how the heart might
strike. Better to leave a trail of crumbs
on the way out, never the way in.

Subhearted

From this view, you're one with the dogs: close, dirty, palms on the ground. Crawl across the room, prone. Look up & imprint what it feels to be small & underbelly as people pass by, legs of motion. Beauty hums in armfuls, hidden flowers, what I lay down, let go—the world & any resolution. Is anyone always on top? Praise tread, the blessing, that gives such clean hands & then lift yourself lifting them off.

How to Care for a Narcissist

He calls again to say he's upset I'm making it
difficult for him to feel close to her. How I
conjure this dissonance—his burled timbre

filling my ear, his want too easily at home.
Of course, it's his erection in the door
I'm trying to close, muscle memory

pushing in. O, the charm. I'm all out of awe.
He's voracious. Carrot & stick, his lashing
out. I mute the phone, ignore his texts

& finally block his number. Sure, I'll miss
the sex: his eyes, my eyes reflecting
pools—*you* & more *you*.

Mezzo

I am the heavy tone
your trouser-role girl, tessitura:
non-castrati witch or bitch, you pick.

My arias are not about me

being about you, Vitruvian butterfly
on Venn's lotus; can you finger this
middle space collision, this marquise

of a vocalise? This melisma *o*—

Lean your ear & fill to the edge,
strings stretch to low & lie
back on the thrum & trill,

the evening's subspace.

Sing me & hold each note
with an open hand, the cognac swirl
of *Louis treize*, the velvet & scratch

of a burning throat.

Mating Season

Barred owls on the river hunt for sex
all night. In a flash mob exchange they pitch
& haggle their charms back & forth into a wild
orangutan vocalise. After such a fury for love
the silence settles, the couplings surely struck.
There's no sleeping through the fireworks
but after, in the absence, the whole night rings
with possibility. Who knows what will come
in the year ahead? Or what to leave behind?
But now I'm awake & thirsty & the half-full
glass at my side is not enough. Too tired
to get out of bed, I close my eyes & lull
against the translation of owls calling out—
If not you, someone. If not you, someone new.

Maenad in America

What some call madness, others call want.
I am tired of sacrifice at the altar

of tradition, the right—

all the merry rituals a sham, displaced
in line, second to a man, third after kids.

Don't ask me to calm down.

Remember the Orpheus misfortune: phallic
in a blur of satyrs, one lyre too many

at the rave. Frenetic, we danced, arms waving,
bodies in constellation, his head still singing.

Blame the god of wine & ecstasy & roofies
& pornified couth. Blame the rape joke,

the patriarchy, those titans—
taxing, trumping, talking heads to flip.

No, I am not on my period. Or your *sugar-
honey-cunt-sweetie-pie*. This is not penis envy

that misogyny warp—

the glass ceiling is a concave mirror,
funhouse hysteria bowling women over,

whose dark circles & rug-burned nerves,
in kitchens & boardrooms, could rip you

a new orifice of light.

Dear Ozy—

I named all my cities for you in this play of civilization,
What You Can't Know (or How Millennia Collapse to Seconds).
I drove to St. Simons & ate dinner at the same table
but not the same meal. Oceans feed tears to oysters—
little tombs of mouth & foot. I knelt in the morning tide
& walked from the King & Prince to the lighthouse,
my ears full of mnemonic song. Even still we fall
through horizon, not unlike a tunnel. Our universe expands

like a black balloon, each life on the bow of its curve.
Dimensions intertwine. The world is full in every space.
A broken nautilus unhands the sequence, subsumes
with sand. Form is just a bottle, but what if we are each other's—
defined by what we fill or what fills us? Unstable rock, tectonic,

what city will rest on you?

Undoll

Some lives grow twisted in the belly, throat
blue & airless. Corset-bound,

I have no arms attached in your packaging
to hold back cellophane, the walls. Boxed.

Your memory trails the way of an elephant, oversized
for a single room. I am strung out, hungry, awake.

Hunger is entropy—ever after. I swallow the night.
I swallow the left side of the bed

& pull the pregnant covers over my eyes
of biding with you. Because you are too much

to swallow. Because yesterday's special is today's
leftover. The tongue diagrams the taste.

I diagram the years—spoon & cup, ocean
& blanket. We have no bones

though I drag you with me. There's nothing
to say now. I remember your hands

calloused & all want. Our whole is
a fractal of everything. I see the pieces.

I see mine coming back
with arms.

Looking at the Lawrence Tree

Georgia O'Keeffe, *The Lawrence Tree*, 1929. Oil on canvas.

standing on its head
the towering pine
frames you
divine
on D.H.'s ranch
& weathered bench
your mind reaching
through branches
& the limn of stars

& midnights
between render
& heaven yearning
canvas your
open arms a sail
across Taos
the blue
the desert wide
that summer of '29

away from the city
& Alfred
& becoming

larger still
looking close
any of all nights
you
just outside
the gilded frame

Hole Reunion Sonnet

Go on take everything, take everything, I want you to.
　　—Hole

Because the nineties are over. We grew up
& put away babydoll grunge & Mary Janes. Because
we heard "Violet" & our girl parts rumored with rage,
rant. Because we were not holes. Who *is* whole?
Our violence was inside. Because we played pretty,
played parts. Because there were holes only we could fill,
but couldn't see. Because good girls don't look for trouble,
but sometimes they do; it finds them. Because we were
more bad than good. Because our mothers lied
& who wants to act doe-eyed coy for some guy? Because
some part of me, maybe the missing part, awoke
on the spot. Because words like *slut* siren, that jaded knife.
Read this & think it's hot. Because hole must mean vagina,
I want to stay naked so you hear me. Because someone will.

Digging Out

Let me wear the day well so when it reaches you, you will enjoy it.
—Sonia Sanchez

before dawn   I wake to let
the dogs outside   no thought   why me
only the day ahead   to wear
hours like a broad grin   brave what the
morning brings   make the day
shine   make tea   & word well
digging deep   into the whole so
you will see   something new when
it was just ground   when what it
wants can be   unhidden   the mind reaches
dark places   the curtained rooms you
hide in   but sun will seek you
out   better to split the stone   it will
give back   put your head down   enjoy
the day   you make it

Equinox

an epithalamium

We live in the pursuit of halcyon,
an elation with wings that will open us
& complement our earthly nakedness.
How we aspire for a blessing, the one
we don't deserve, even on our best day,
the one who will hold us in the snow
in green mountains & in Paris taxis,
laughing & sharing cigarettes & Serifos.
We live for a patient ear, for the keeper
of blue secrets & our whole, long lives.
We look up believing—how we live
for a song-wide smile across the table,
Pangaea with never the sea between,
the day & night equal & luminous.

Notes

p 7   Mitochondria passes female to female through generations, making "mtDNA Eve" the most recent common matrilineal ancestor of all living people.

p 9   The line, "You know that I'm no good" is borrowed from Amy Winehouse's song of the same name (2006).

p 19   "The Unfaithful Housewife" is a reply to the poem of the same name by Federico García Lorca, translated by Conor O'Callaghan, and published in *Poetry* (2011).

p 21   "Duchess" is a reference to Robert Browning's poem "My Last Duchess" (1842).

p 41   *for Doug*

p 50   The italicized lines are borrowed from one of Rizzo's solos in *Grease* (1978): "There Are Worse Things I Could Do," words and music by Warren Casey and Jim Jacobs.

p 52   "As Faithful as His Options" is in conversation with *The House of Mirth* (1905) by Edith Wharton from which it borrows its italicized lines. The title is a reference to a Chris Rock joke.

p 59   "Wuthering" is a reference to *Wuthering Heights* (1847) by
        Emily Brontë.

p 64   "Hard Habit to Break" is a reference to a 1984 song by Chicago.

p 65   Of over 200 silhouettes in Ana Mendieta's series, *Siluetas* (1973–
        78), the poem most directly references the image of *Untitled*
        (1976) in juxtaposition with her death and the parallels. The
        epigraph is from an artist statement (1981).

p 68   "Closing Stepford" is a reference to the Ira Levin novel, *The
        Stepford Wives*, as well as the movie adaptations by directors
        Bryan Forbes (1975) and Frank Oz (2004).

p 79   "Mirror, Mirror" is in conversation with Brenda Shaughnessy's
        poem "Postfeminism" (1999) from which it borrows
        several tropes.

p 82   Tessitura is the comfortable range of a singer. Castrati were
        males with singing voices equivalent to a mezzo-soprano;
        castration before puberty produced the castrato voice.
        "Vitruvian butterfly" refers to Leonardo di Vinci's *Vitruvian
        Man* (1490). *Louis treize* is a slang reference to *Louis XIII* de
        Rémy Martin, a luxury cognac.

p 86   "Dear Ozy—" is a reference to "Ozymandias" (1818) by Percy
        Bysshe Shelley.

p 92   "Digging Out" uses the golden shovel form but borrows its
        embedded line from one of Sonia Sanchez's haikus in *Homegirls
        and Handgrenades* (1984).

p 93   *for Didi & Major*

About the Section Titles

I have ridden in your cart, driver,
waved my nude arms at villages going by,
learning **the last bright routes**, survivor

    —— ANNE SEXTON
      from "Her Kind"

so many things seem filled with **the intent
to be lost** that their loss is no disaster.

    —— ELIZABETH BISHOP
      from "One Art"

You will not listen
to resistance, you cover me

with flags, **a dark red
season**, you delete from me
all other colours

    —— MARGARET ATWOOD
      from "Hesitations Outside the Door"

the thing I came for:
the wreck and not the story of the wreck
the thing itself and **not the myth**
the drowned face always staring
toward the sun

— ADRIENNE RICH
from "Diving into the Wreck"

Acknowledgments

My deepest gratitude to the editors of the following publications in which these poems first appeared, often in earlier versions or under different titles:

2 Horatio: "Digging Out"
The Adroit Journal: "Undoll," "Little Wekiva River," "What's Bottled Breaks"
AGNI: "Lethe," "Mating Season"
Anomaly: "Gaslight"
Apalachee Review: "Mitochrondrial Eve in Reverse"
Bayou: "The Line of a Girl"
The Cape Horn: "Magnolia"
Colorado Review: "Portrait of a Clarion"
Cordite Poetry Review: "Wuthering"
Dead Mule of Southern Literature: "There are Days," "Waiting," "South Charlene"
Diode Poetry Journal: "Ripe," "Rizzo's Song," "Newlywed"
The Ekphrastic Review: "Tomb of the Wrestlers"
Fjords Review: "Patience as a Force," "Oblation"
The Florida Review: "Stupefied," "Cage Sonnet"
Foundry: "Waterline"
Fugue: "Here is Somewhere"
Green Mountains Review: "Mirror, Mirror," "The Last Silueta"
Hayden's Ferry Review: "To Come Undone"
Iron Horse Review: "Maenad in America"

JuxtaProse: "Matryoshka"

LEVELER: "The Google Earth Effect"

The Literary Review: "Mall at Millennia," "Why Not Minot"

The Los Angeles Review: "Hole Reunion Sonnet"

Louisiana Cultural Vistas: "Letter to My Embryo, Evolving"

The Massachusetts Review: "Mezzo"

The Mississippi Review: "After Fifteen Years"

The Missouri Review: "As Faithful as His Options"

Moria: "Closing Stepford," "Sunday School," "Post-Hellenic"

The Offing: "Third Wave"

New Ohio Review: "Facebook Sonnet"

New South: "Phalaenopsis"

Painted Bride Quarterly: "The Unfaithful Housewife," "Duchess,"
    "Dear Ozy—"

Ploughshares: "Lot's Wife Leaves Suburbia"

Plume: "The Path of Non-Attachment"

Post Road: "In Elixir," "Rewind"

Prairie Schooner: "Doll, House"

Salamander: "A Sting Hovers in My Window"

Spillway: "Loaded Noir"

Split Lip Magazine: "How to Care for a Narcissist"

Tinderbox Poetry Journal: "Black Iris Sonnet," "Equinox"

WSQ: Women's Studies Quarterly: "If Barbie had a Brain"

"Lethe" won an Academy of American Poets Prize and appears on *Poets. org.* "Looking at the Lawrence Tree" also won an Academy of American Poets Prize.

"The Line of a Girl" won the 2016 Tennessee Williams/New Orleans Literary Festival Poetry Prize, selected by Yusef Komunyakaa.

"Matryoshka" was anthologized in *Borderlands & Crossroads: Writing the Motherland,* Demeter Press, 2016.

Several poems were written as a part of the Tupelo 30/30 Project, January 2016.

"Lethe" and "Mating Season" also appeared in *Barrow Street*; "What's Bottled Breaks," "In Elixir," and "To Come Undone" also appeared in *WSQ: Women's Studies Quarterly;* "Doll, House" also appeared in *Sugar House Review*; "Letter to My Embryo, Evolving" and "Third Wave" also appeared in *Canadian Woman Studies*; "Waterline" was reprinted and featured as a part of the *poems2go* mobile poetry journal funded by a grant from The Witter Brynner Foundation.

—

My gratitude to all those who've walked alongside. I name many here but could easily name others. *Thank you.*

To Eleanor Boudreau, whose brilliance helped order this book. To Sandra Chávez Johnson, for fierce, abiding friendship and wisdom. To Didi Jackson and Michele Parker Randall, for umpteen mornings and summers of poetry and laughter. To Yolanda Franklin, for her inspiration and light. To KMA Sullivan, for her insights and true believing—and to everyone at YesYes Books.

To Carol Frost, Barbara Hamby, Major Jackson, and James Kimbrell, for each honoring me with their time, honesty, and high expectations.

To those who shared their encouragement, comments, and kindness. Above and beyond thanks to Jennifer Adams, Vidhu Aggarwal, Kaveh Akbar, Bruce Aufhammer, Erin Belieu, Kelly Butler, Marianne Chan, Billy Collins, Suzannah Gilman Collins, Dorsey Craft, David Daniel, Mary Ann de Stefano, Andrew Epstein, Jill Alexander Essbaum, William Fargason, Gwen Figueroa, Kathleen Graber, Erin Hoover, Joan Houlihan, Jessie King, David Kirby, Paige Lewis, Susan Lilley, Timothy Liu, Janet Manuel-Atwater, Brandi Nicole Martin, Alice Mattison, Kirsten Miles, Rita Mookerjee, Lee Patterson, Dustin Pearson, Ruth Polleys, Diane Roberts, Bob Shacochis, Jeff Shotts, Robert Stilling, Barrett Warner, Josh Wild, Cocoa Williams, Mark Wunderlich, and Josephine Yu. And to Ellen Heller, Cheryl Iverson, and Barbara Vadas, for their early encouragement.

To Ian, for waking me (twice). To Geoff, for a thousand walks and always. To Peggy, for her deep understanding.

To my parents, Teresa and Alfred, for love beyond. To my brother, Joel. To Thomas. To Molly. To the memories of Joyce, Sadie, Ada, Rachel, Mama Red, and my ancestors—*You are always in the room.*

And to Douglas, Morgan, and Lara—*love times infinity.*

TANYA GRAE was born in South Carolina and raised across America as her family moved with military reassignments. She earned an MFA from Bennington College and is the recipient of two Academy of American Poets Prizes and a Kingsbury Fellowship. She was a National Poetry Series finalist and her poem "The Line of a Girl" won the Tennessee Williams/New Orleans Literary Festival Poetry Prize, selected by Yusef Komunyakaa. She lives in Tallahassee and teaches at Florida State University while finishing her PhD. Her work has been published in such journals as *Ploughshares, American Poetry Review, AGNI, Prairie Schooner*, and *Post Road*.

Also from YesYes Books

A New Language for Falling Out of Love by Meghan Privitello

I'm So Fine: A List of Famous Men & What I Had On by Khadijah Queen

American Barricade by Danniel Schoonebeek

The Anatomist by Taryn Schwilling

Gilt by Raena Shirali

Panic Attack, USA by Nate Slawson

[insert] boy by Danez Smith

Man vs Sky by Corey Zeller

The Bones of Us by J. Bradley
　　[Art by Adam Scott Mazer]

CHAPBOOK COLLECTIONS

Vinyl 45s

　　After by Fatimah Asghar

　　Inside My Electric City by Caylin Capra-Thomas

　　Dream with a Glass Chamber by Aricka Foreman

　　Exit Pastoral by Aidan Forster

　　Pepper Girl by Jonterri Gadson

　　Of Darkness and Tumbling by Mónica Gomery

　　Bad Star by Rebecca Hazelton

　　Makeshift Cathedral by Peter LaBerge

　　Still, the Shore by Keith Leonard

　　Please Don't Leave Me Scarlett Johansson by Thomas Patrick Levy

　　Juned by Jenn Marie Nunes

　　A History of Flamboyance by Justin Phillip Reed

　　Unmonstrous by John Allen Taylor

　　Giantess by Emily Vizzo

　　No by Ocean Vuong

　　This American Ghost by Michael Wasson

Blue Note Editions

 Beastgirl & Other Origin Myths by Elizabeth Acevedo

 Kissing Caskets by Mahogany L. Browne

 One Above One Below: Positions & Lamentations
  by Gala Mukomolova

Companion Series

 Inadequate Grave by Brandon Courtney

 The Rest of the Body by Jay Deshpande